TUDOR

Triptych of the Royal Arms

ELIZABETHA MAGNA REGINA ANGLIÆ

The Great Bible of 1539

Pestle and mortar

Tudor nobleman

Mary Queen of Scots' rosary and prayer book

Thumbscrew

Beheading sword

Roasted peacock

King
Henry VIII

Queen
Elizabeth I

DK EYEWITNESS GUIDES

TUDOR

Written by
SIMON ADAMS

Tudor
noblewoman

Silk embroidered mittens, given by Elizabeth I to one of her maids

LONDON, NEW YORK,
MELBOURNE, MUNICH, DELHI

Rosary beads with medals

Parsley

Lungwort

Editor Bradley Round
Art editors Joanne Connor, Leah Germann, Joanne Little
Senior editor Carey Scott
Senior art editor Stefan Podhorodecki
Managing editor Andrew Macintyre
Managing art editor Jane Thomas
Production controller Rochelle Talary
Special photography Andy Crawford, Dave King
Picture researcher Jo de Gray
Picture librarians Sarah Mills, Karl Stange
DTP designer Siu Yin Ho
Jacket designer Simon Oon

Consultant
Dr Lucy Wooding,
King's College, London

Queen Elizabeth's locket ring

First published in Great Britain in 2004 by
Dorling Kindersley Limited,
80 Strand, London WC2R ORL

A CIP catalogue record for this book is
available from the British Library.

ISBN 1 4053 0474 X

Colour reproduction by Colourscan, Singapore
Printed in China by Toppan Printing Co.,
(Shenzhen) Ltd.

Tudor street trader

The Armada jewel

See our complete
catalogue at

www.dk.com

Contents

Tudor
noblewoman

Who were the Tudors?

In 1485, A NEW FAMILY, or dynasty, of rulers seized the throne of England. The Tudors ruled until 1603, producing two of England's most colourful and successful monarchs, Henry VIII and Elizabeth I. Yet they might never have ascended to the throne. From 1154–1399, England had been ruled by a family called the Plantaganets. Then the crown was taken by the Lancaster family but, in 1455, a rival family, the Yorks, threatened the throne. Fighting broke out between them, and their battles became known as the Wars of the Roses. The Tudors inherited the Lancastrian claim when most of the Lancaster family was killed. In 1485, Henry Tudor defeated the Yorkist king Richard III in battle and became King Henry VII.

JOHN OF GAUNT
Henry Tudor's claim to the throne lay on his mother's side. Her great-grandfather was the fourth son of King Edward III, John of Gaunt. As Duke of Lancaster, John of Gaunt was a powerful figure in 14th-century England.

WARS OF THE ROSES
Ten major battles and a few minor skirmishes were fought during the 30-year-long Wars of the Roses – essentially a family quarrel between the royal houses of Lancaster and York. The wars finally ended when the Lancastrian claimant, Henry Tudor, defeated and killed the Yorkist king, Richard III, in battle at Bosworth Field in Leicestershire on 22 August 1485.

The Tudor Royal Family Tree

Tudor rose denotes reign of Tudor monarch

Arthur
d. 1502

Henry VIII
1509-1547

Mary 1
1553-1558

Elizabeth 1
1558-1603

Edward VI
1547-1553

Both the Lancastrian and Yorkist armies were supplemented by paid soldiers, or mercenaries

More than 80 nobles lost their lives during the Wars of the Roses

One of the 10 battles of the Wars of the Roses

Henry VII
🌹 1485-1509

Margaret

James V of Scotland

Mary Queen of Scots

Mary

Frances

Lady Jane Grey

James 1 (VI of Scotland)
1603-1625

Rose: Red and White, from a 16th-century botanical book

More than 17,000 pieces of stained glass make up the Rose Window

The Rose Window at York Minster

The Tudor rose decorates the window

A NEW ROSE

The Wars of the Roses were named after the emblems used by the royal houses of Lancaster and York – a red rose for Lancaster and a white rose for York. After becoming king, Henry Tudor married Elizabeth of York, uniting the two rival houses. Henry combined the white rose of York with the red rose of Lancaster to make a new emblem, the Tudor rose. The great Rose Window in the south transept of York Minster commemorates this marriage and the subsequent union of the York and Lancaster families and the new Tudor dynasty.

Cylindrical great tower dominates the castle

Outer defensive walls

Henry was born in this tower

WELSH CONNECTION

Henry Tudor was born here, at Pembroke Castle, Wales, in 1457. Then Earl of Richmond, Henry had only a distant claim to the throne but, in time, the lack of other suitable claimants increased his importance. By 1471, he was a real threat to the throne and his uncle took him to Brittany, France, for his own protection. Henry's Welsh heritage was important to him – he landed in Wales to claim his throne in 1485 and most of his troops at Bosworth were Welsh. It is probable that he had spent only a few weeks in total in England before he became its king.

The first Tudor king

HENRY VII WAS A SHREWD MAN who, having seized the throne by force, kept it through the subtle use of royal power and strong government. Suspicious and insecure, he was the first English king to have his own personal bodyguard, the Yeoman of the Guard (still on duty today at the Tower of London). But Henry was a successful king, building up the national finances, encouraging trade, and largely keeping England out of foreign entanglements. When he died in 1509, England was the most peaceful and prosperous it had been for half a century.

THE ROYAL UNION
Henry's wife Elizabeth of York was the sister of Edward V, who was deposed before his coronation could take place, in 1483, and probably murdered. Although theirs was a marriage of political convenience, uniting the rival houses of York and Lancaster, it was also a love match. The couple had eight children, and Henry was devastated when Elizabeth died shortly after the birth of their final daughter in February 1503.

ROYAL IMPOSTERS
During Henry's reign, two impostors tried to seize the throne with Yorkist support. The first, Lambert Simnel, claimed to be the nephew of Edward IV, but was easily defeated. The second, Perkin Warbeck (left), claimed to be a long-lost brother of Elizabeth of York, and caused Henry considerable trouble until he was finally captured and executed in 1499.

SECURING PEACE
Flags like this were used to rally knights and soldiers on the battlefield during the Wars of the Roses. Henry was determined to break the power of the warlike English nobles by banning them from raising their own personal armies. This helped end the recurring civil wars between members of the royal family.

PATRON OF THE ARTS
Henry was a learned and cultured man. He encouraged French and Italian scholars and artists to come to England, bringing the latest ideas from the new spirit of learning, which would become known as the Renaissance. Among them was the famous Italian sculptor Pietro Torrigiano (1472–1528), who made this bust of Henry.

RICHMOND PALACE
Henry had a number of royal palaces to live in, but his favourite was Richmond Palace, built on the site of Sheen Palace by the River Thames in Surrey, which had burned down in 1499. Henry died here in 1509, as did Elizabeth I almost a century later.

The red rose of Lancaster, which was united with the white rose of York by the royal marriage

THRIFTY POLICIES

When Henry became king, England was almost bankrupt because of the civil wars of preceding years. Through careful nurturing of the royal finances – he personally checked and signed every page of his own household's accounts – he built up a substantial income and left the crown in surplus at his death. Henry's policies were not popular though. His two main tax collectors were put to death a year after Henry died, to considerable popular acclaim.

The Tax Collector by Marinus Roejmerswaalen

King Henrye the seventh

ENCOURAGING BOOKS

Henry and his wife were both keen supporters of England's first printer, William Caxton (1420–91). In 1476, Caxton printed the first edition of Geoffrey Chaucer's poem *The Canterbury Tales*. Above is his 1483 second edition, which had illustrations added. The stories of pilgrims on their way to Canterbury proved very popular, and the book is still read today.

Caxton's trademark

HENRY'S DEATH

Henry died in April 1509 and was buried beside his wife in Westminster Abbey, the final resting place of all Tudor monarchs except Henry VIII. Although respected as a king, Henry was not loved. At his funeral, John Fisher, Bishop of Rochester, acknowledged that, "King Henry, if thou were alive again, many one that is here present now would pretend a full great pity and tenderness upon thee!"

NEW WORLDS DISCOVERED

In 1492, the Italian navigator Christopher Columbus (1451–1506) stumbled upon the islands of the Caribbean, while in search of a new westerly sea route to Asia. Columbus's voyage attracted huge attention in England, and Henry joined in the enthusiasm, sponsoring the voyages of the Cabots to North America in 1497 (pp. 36–37).

The Santa Maria, Columbus's flagship

Tudor England

IN 1500, THE POPULATION of England was a mere 2.6 million. London was the only major city, and most people lived in small market towns or in isolated rural areas. Tudor society was divided into three main classes: a small nobility, a larger professional and middle class, and a big working class of skilled craftsmen, farm workers, servants, and labourers. Travel was much more uncommon than it is today. Few left the district in which they were born and foreign journeys were extremely rare.

HARD LABOUR
The vast majority of people in Tudor England worked as agricultural labourers, or husbandmen, on farms owned by wealthy landowners. A few were yeoman farmers, owning their own small plot of land which they worked as a family business. Husbandmen received a weekly wage, part of which might have been paid in clothing, food, and drink.

WOOL TRADE
The export of woollen cloth to Europe was the most valuable overseas trade of its day, rising by more than 60 per cent during Henry VII's reign alone. Most farmers therefore kept sheep, but this eventually led to a shortage of crops.

Hand-spun woollen cloth trousers

Pitchfork

Scythe

FARMING THE LAND
The crops Tudor farmers grew were similar to those grown today, and included wheat, barley, oats, peas, beans, and root crops. They also kept cattle, pigs, and poultry. Farmers worked the land by hand, ploughing the fields with teams of oxen or horses and making their own tools.

THE FARMER'S WIFE
The life of a farmer's wife was busy and hard. On top of the normal household chores, she had to make butter, cheese, and beer, collect eggs, apples, and other fruit, and make clothes for her family. She could supplement the family income by selling any excess produce.

Houses had wooden frames filled in with whitewashed brick or thin wood

MEETING AND TRADING
Market towns were the focus point of rural life. On the hustle and bustle of market day they were a meeting place for farmers, traders, and craftworkers from across the county selling and exchanging their goods. Over half the total population of England lived in the major market towns.

MERRY ENGLAND

Weddings were celebrated with great gusto, as the painting of this wedding party in Bermondsey, (now in south London, but then still a village) shows. Guests contributed food and drink to the feast, and brought their own musical instruments. A good wedding party might start before the happy couple had even got to the church, and could continue for days.

Beards became fashionable after the reign of Henry VIII

THE MIDDLE CLASS

The landowners, merchants, professionals such as lawyers, and others who made up the middle class were the backbone of Tudor England. They served in the government, enforced the law as justices of the peace, and sat in parliament. Many lived in small manor houses on their estates, or in well-appointed town houses.

Glass windows were a recent innovation, and extremely expensive, when this house was built

Hardwick Hall, Derbyshire

NOBLE HOUSES

The nobility lived in ancestral castles or in later years, country houses with dozens of bedrooms. Hardwick Hall, built in the 1590s as a deliberate display of wealth, is one such house. It was described as "more glass than wall" because of its huge windows, which let lots of light into the spacious interior.

A middle-class man could afford small luxuries, such as this fur-panelled overcoat

THE NOBILITY

At the start of the Tudor period, the aristocracy consisted of just 38 noble families. Most held great power locally as landowners and employers of rural labour. Their wives and daughters were well provided for, living in considerable luxury with fine clothes and numerous servants to look after them.

Food and feasting

THE ENGLISH HAD A REPUTATION for gluttony among their continental peers. The rich did enjoy large, expensive meals, but they were as much for show as for consumption. Henry VIII once gave a ten-course banquet for a visiting ambassador that lasted more than seven hours. Even ordinary people ate better than their European cousins. A vast array of food was available from within England, and overseas trade meant that goods such as sugar and spices were imported, though these were expensive. Leftovers from sumptuous meals were passed on to the servants to take what they wanted and give the rest to the poor, who gathered around the gates of noble houses.

TUDOR KITCHEN
The Tudor kitchen was a place to cook, eat, and socialize. Grander kitchens had large ovens and adjoining sculleries, cold stores for meat, bakeries, and wine cellars. Poorer kitchens were less ostentatious, and often had no oven, but whatever their size, all were dominated by the open fire used for boiling large cauldrons of water, roasting meats and birds on a rotating spit, and cooking stews and other dishes.

PEACOCK ON A PLATE
At a Tudor feast, it was just as important for each dish to look spectacular as well as taste delicious. "Peacock royal" was a particularly popular dish. A peacock was skinned, stuffed with dried fruits and spices, cooked, and then placed back inside its feathered skin. Tudor cooks would also have been required to stuff swans, bake porpoise pie, and roast blackbirds and larks.

Mint

Sage

Parsley

Thyme

Rosemary

FLAVOURING
Herbs were widely used to season food and drink, as well as being used in medicines. They were collected locally from the wild or grown in gardens alongside flowers and vegetables. Rich people had specially created herb gardens.

Crystal wine glass presented to Elizabeth I

EASY EATING
Most knives in England came from Sheffield, where they had been manufactured since the 1300s. Even in the noblest house, food was cut up with a knife and then eaten with the fingers. Forks were not introduced until the end of the sixteenth century.

CLASSY GLASSES
Wine glasses were fashionable in the homes of the rich and noble. They were imported from Venice, Italy, making them a very expensive luxury. Goblets were more commonly made of wood, pewter, or silver and, very rarely, gold.

SILVER SPOONS
The poor used wooden spoons, but rich people had spoons of pewter or silver. These might be engraved with the family coat of arms or carry an emblem or figure at the top of the handle. Owning an engraved silver spoon was a way of proclaiming one's wealth and status in society. Some people carried their own spoons about with them.

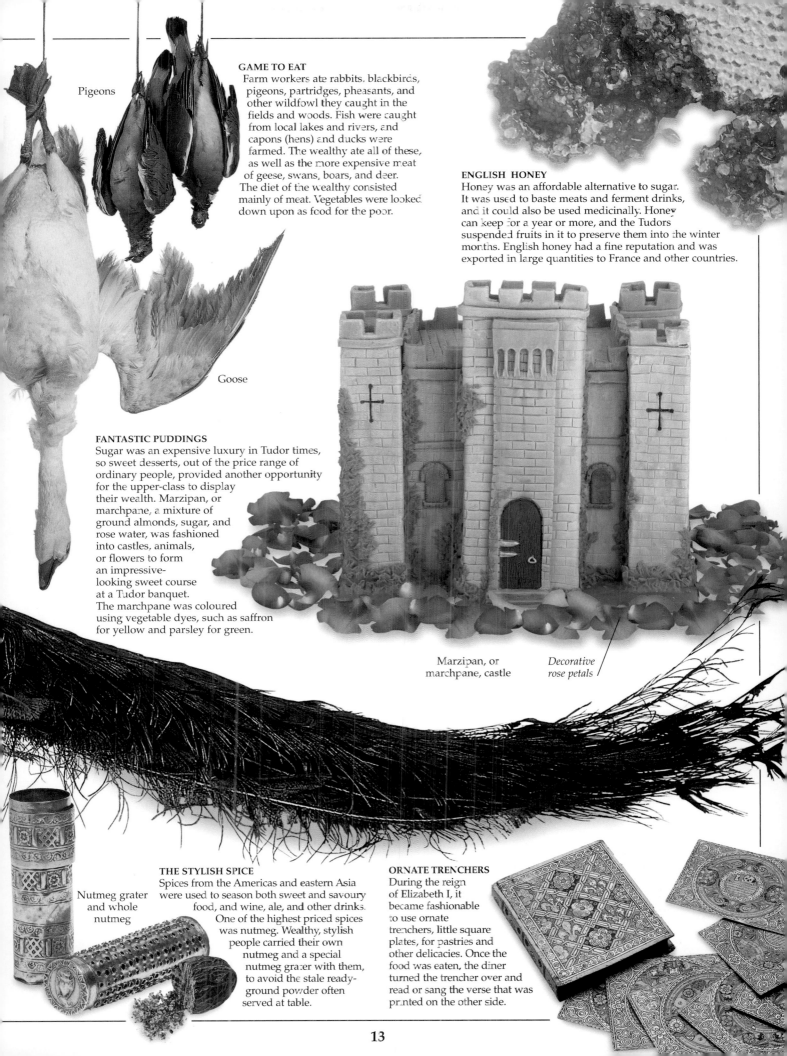

GAME TO EAT

Farm workers ate rabbits, blackbirds, pigeons, partridges, pheasants, and other wildfowl they caught in the fields and woods. Fish were caught from local lakes and rivers, and capons (hens) and ducks were farmed. The wealthy ate all of these, as well as the more expensive meat of geese, swans, boars, and deer. The diet of the wealthy consisted mainly of meat. Vegetables were looked down upon as food for the poor.

Pigeons

Goose

ENGLISH HONEY

Honey was an affordable alternative to sugar. It was used to baste meats and ferment drinks, and it could also be used medicinally. Honey can keep for a year or more, and the Tudors suspended fruits in it to preserve them into the winter months. English honey had a fine reputation and was exported in large quantities to France and other countries.

FANTASTIC PUDDINGS

Sugar was an expensive luxury in Tudor times, so sweet desserts, out of the price range of ordinary people, provided another opportunity for the upper-class to display their wealth. Marzipan, or marchpane, a mixture of ground almonds, sugar, and rose water, was fashioned into castles, animals, or flowers to form an impressive-looking sweet course at a Tudor banquet. The marchpane was coloured using vegetable dyes, such as saffron for yellow and parsley for green.

Marzipan, or marchpane, castle

Decorative rose petals

THE STYLISH SPICE

Spices from the Americas and eastern Asia were used to season both sweet and savoury food, and wine, ale, and other drinks. One of the highest priced spices was nutmeg. Wealthy, stylish people carried their own nutmeg and a special nutmeg grater with them, to avoid the stale ready-ground powder often served at table.

Nutmeg grater and whole nutmeg

ORNATE TRENCHERS

During the reign of Elizabeth I, it became fashionable to use ornate trenchers, little square plates, for pastries and other delicacies. Once the food was eaten, the diner turned the trencher over and read or sang the verse that was printed on the other side.

The court of Henry VIII

HENRY VIII SUCCEEDED HIS FATHER Henry VII to the throne in 1509, aged 17. Many welcomed his accession, especially those nobles and merchants who had been persecuted and heavily taxed by his father. Henry VIII's style of kingship was flamboyant, and he hoped to make an impact – through both war and diplomacy – on the European stage. Henry was also devoted to pleasure. He made his court a centre of intellectual and artistic activity, and enjoyed sports, music and dancing, and lavish banquets. His extravagant lifestyle wasted much of the money Henry's prudent father had saved.

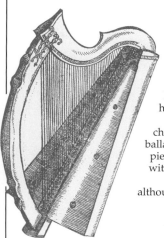

CURRENT AFFAIRS
The Dutch scholar Desiderius Erasmus (c.1467–1536) was one of Europe's leading intellectuals, writing extensively on religious affairs and education. A visitor to Henry's court, he did much to introduce new ideas and learning to England.

The Ambassadors, by Hans Holbein, 1533

Thomas Wolsey in his red cardinal's robes

Padded shoulders emphasize an imposing physique

THE RENAISSANCE IN ENGLAND
Henry VII had shown interest in the ideas of the Renaissance, but his son did more to bring the new learning to England. His intellectual curiosity led him to support many Renaissance scholars and artists. This masterpiece by Hans Holbein (c.1497–1543), Henry's court artist, depicts two diplomats with some of the latest scientific instruments of the day.

RISE AND FALL OF WOLSEY
The first advisor to the King was Thomas Wolsey (1475–1529). The son of an Ipswich butcher, Wolsey rose through the Church to become Archbishop of York in 1514 and Cardinal a year later. As Chancellor of England from 1515, he managed the affairs of state for Henry with great skill, amassing huge wealth for himself in the process. He fell out of the King's favour in 1529, but died before he could be tried for treason.

HENRY'S MUSIC
As a youth, Henry learned to play several musical instruments, including the organ, the virginals (a type of harpsichord), the lute, and the harp, all to a high standard. He also composed music, writing church masses and 18 songs and ballads, as well as 15 instrumental pieces. His name has been linked with *Greensleeves*, one of the most famous of English folk songs, although there is no direct evidence that Henry was its composer.

A harp of the Tudor period

Pastime with good company, one of many songs composed by Henry

Fine jewels, a display of wealth

Detail from the Westminster Tournament Roll, showing a royal joust

A SPORTING LIFE
Henry was addicted to sport, and especially enjoyed riding and jousting (p. 44). Jousting tournaments were held at court on important holy days and on special occasions, such as the birth of a royal prince, or the visit of a foreign envoy. The illustration above shows Henry jousting before his first wife Catherine of Aragon, in 1512, to celebrate the birth of his first son, Henry. His joy at having a son was short-lived, for the child died when just three months old.

Hooded falcon

HUNTING AND HAWKING
When he was not jousting, Henry hunted stags or, when hunting stopped for the winter, hawked with falcons bred specially for the sport. Most of Henry's youth was spent in the saddle, leaving him little time for anything else. The Tudor chronicler, Edward Hall, wrote of 1526 that "because all this summer the King took his pastime in hunting, ... nothing happened worthy to be written of."

Ceremonial dagger

Fine gold thread

Field of the Cloth-of-gold

Portrait of Henry VIII by Hans Holbein, 1537

FOREIGN POLICY
Henry's policy towards France, England's old enemy, veered between friendship and open warfare. After invading France in 1513, Henry made peace and within a year had married his sister Mary to the French king, Louis XII. More years of war followed until 1520, when Wolsey organized a meeting between Henry and the new king, Francis I, to sign a treaty of friendship. They met at the Field of the Cloth-of-gold, so-called because of the richly decorated tents erected there. But, two years later, they were at war again.

KINGLY STATURE
The young king was an imposing man, standing 193 cm (6 ft 4 in) tall, with broad shoulders, fair skin, and red hair, but with a high-pitched, thin voice. He was highly intelligent and, as well as enjoying sport and music, wrote books on religious theory, or theology, and revelled in intellectual debate. In his youth he was physically fit but a lifetime of eating and drinking heavily took its toll and, in his later years, he became so fat that a special machine was needed to haul him upstairs.

Henry rides to meet the French king

A harsh life

FOR MOST PEOPLE in Tudor England, life was far from easy. If infancy was survived, an array of deadly diseases threatened to cut lives short. Medicine was primitive, and doctors and surgeons did little to improve the situation. The average life expectancy was only about 35 years. For those unlucky or desperate enough to fall foul of the law, punishment was cruel. Petty crime brought humiliation or whipping. Serious crime was often punished by a gruesome death, and torture awaited anyone unlucky enough to find themselves in the Tower of London accused of treason.

BRIEF CHILDHOOD
Out of every 100 Tudor babies born, only 70 reached their first birthday and perhaps only 50 saw the age of five. Typhus, smallpox, and other deadly diseases were a constant threat. Here, a toddler is dragged away from his family by Death, depicted as a skeleton.

Cauterising iron

TREATING THE PLAGUE
The boils of plague victims were cauterised, or sterilized, with a red-hot iron. This treated the symptoms but did nothing to address the disease itself. The plague was untreatable, and could be contained only by segregating the affected and leaving them to die.

Marjoram healed bruises and swellings

Long-nosed mask for a snoop or meddler

MASKS OF SHAME
For anti-social behaviour such as gossiping or nosiness, the punishment was usually humiliation. The offenders were made to walk through the streets wearing comical masks that mocked their crime, and endure ridicule from the townspeople. Some masks used to punish gossips went beyond humiliation. These had a spike-covered mouthpiece that entered the mouth to cause severe injury.

Feverfew for headaches and childbirth

MEDICINAL HERBS
A wide range of herbs were used in medicine. Some were fanciful, but many, such as lemon balm, are still used today. Herbalists played a similar role to present-day doctors. They had a better reputation than surgeons, who were thought to be more interested in making money than in medicine.

Lemon balm for most ailments and illnesses

Pomander – container for aromatic herbs

PREVENTATIVE PERFUME
People carried pomanders in the vain hope that the sweet smell would ward off bubonic plague. The plague struck several times in the Tudor period, but it hit with a vengeance in 1563–64, when 17,000 people died in London – about one-sixth of the city's population.

Lungwort to treat chest disorders

Tudor
whipping flail

Flail to whip beggar

Scavenger's
Daughter

WHIPPED OUT OF TOWN
Tudor governments believed in helping the
deserving poor, but able-bodied people who
preferred to beg or steal rather than work
were punished. This beggar has been found
guilty of vagrancy: his punishment is a public
whipping through the streets.

TORTURE DEVICES
Prisoners at the Tower of London
were faced with at least seven
different torture devices. One was
the Scavenger's Daughter, or
Skevington's Gyves, named after
Henry VIII's Lieutenant of the Tower,
Sir Henry Skevington. This metal
band was wrapped round the victim
and tightened by a giant screw, forcing
him to crouch with his shoulders close
to his knees. In comparison,
thumbscrews were
relatively painless.

Thumb
Screw

Mask for
a gossip

Naked sinners guarded by devils

SENTENCED TO DEATH
Murder, manslaughter, treason,
stealing hawks, witchcraft,
highway robbery, and desertion
in the field of battle were all
crimes punishable by death.
High-ranking people were
beheaded, but commoners
were hanged. In London,
the public hangman
dispatched about
300 people a year.

GRUESOME WARNING
The heads of traitors
executed in London were
stuck on sticks and placed on
London Bridge as a warning to others.
In 1599, a visitor from Switzerland saw
more than 30 in place. He was astonished
that the young Earl of Surrey took pride in the
fact that his late grandfather's was one of them!

TORMENTS OF HELL
Hell was a real and terrifying place to most
people in Tudor England, whether Protestant
or Catholic. The Church taught that when a
person died, the good and bad deeds of their
life were weighed by God. Eternal damnation
in the fiery flames awaited anyone whose sins
outweighed their good deeds.

Defence of the kingdom

Soldier using early firearm

IN THE CENTURY BETWEEN the seizure of the throne by Henry Tudor and the defeat of the Spanish Armada, England was frequently threatened with invasion by Scotland, Ireland, France, and the Netherlands. It also often faced internal dissent. Defence was, therefore, a major preoccupation of Tudor governments, and the art of warfare developed considerably. By the end of the Tudor period, traditional longbows, lances, and swords had given way to firearms. The use of cannons had changed the design of forts, which now had to be stocky and rounded to withstand and deflect the new firepower.

Reinforced breastplate for protection against firearms

Plates could t lowere allow to the j

THE BATTLE OF FLODDEN
In 1513, James IV of Scotland, husband of Henry VIII's sister Margaret, invaded England after Henry attacked France, an ally of the Scots. James was killed fighting the English at the Battle of Flodden in Northumberland, along with most of the Scottish nobility. In 1542, his son James V invaded Engand. His army too was defeated, at the Battle of Solway Moss.

UNLUCKY MARY ROSE
The pride of Henry VIII's navy was the *Mary Rose*, built in 1509–10. One of the most advanced ships of its time, it was believed that no town in the world could withstand its firepower of 207 guns. Ironically, in 1545 during a naval battle with the French, a sudden gust of wind heeled the ship over. Water poured in through the open lower gunports and the ship capsized and sank, drowning 470 men.

A model of the Tudor warship the *Mary Rose*

Tools used in shipbuilding

SHIPBUILDING
Henry's demand for a modern, powerful navy led to the establishment of the world's first dry dock at Deptford, on the Thames. Others soon followed. Hundreds of shipwrights were employed to build the ships, using the latest technique for making the hulls. Wood for the hulls came from the oak forests surrounding London.

Plates allow knee to bend

Armour was made from steel

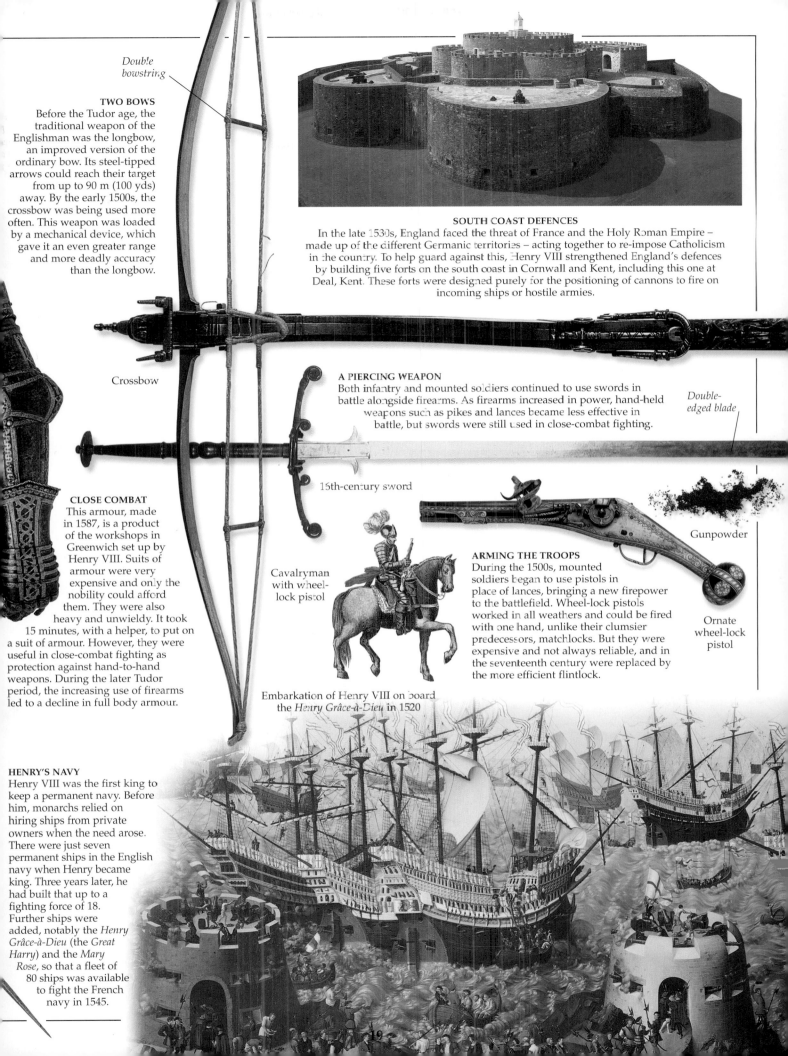

TWO BOWS

Before the Tudor age, the traditional weapon of the Englishman was the longbow, an improved version of the ordinary bow. Its steel-tipped arrows could reach their target from up to 90 m (100 yds) away. By the early 1500s, the crossbow was being used more often. This weapon was loaded by a mechanical device, which gave it an even greater range and more deadly accuracy than the longbow.

Double bowstring

Crossbow

SOUTH COAST DEFENCES

In the late 1530s, England faced the threat of France and the Holy Roman Empire – made up of the different Germanic territories – acting together to re-impose Catholicism in the country. To help guard against this, Henry VIII strengthened England's defences by building five forts on the south coast in Cornwall and Kent, including this one at Deal, Kent. These forts were designed purely for the positioning of cannons to fire on incoming ships or hostile armies.

A PIERCING WEAPON

Both infantry and mounted soldiers continued to use swords in battle alongside firearms. As firearms increased in power, hand-held weapons such as pikes and lances became less effective in battle, but swords were still used in close-combat fighting.

Double-edged blade

15th-century sword

CLOSE COMBAT

This armour, made in 1587, is a product of the workshops in Greenwich set up by Henry VIII. Suits of armour were very expensive and only the nobility could afford them. They were also heavy and unwieldy. It took 15 minutes, with a helper, to put on a suit of armour. However, they were useful in close-combat fighting as protection against hand-to-hand weapons. During the later Tudor period, the increasing use of firearms led to a decline in full body armour.

Cavalryman with wheel-lock pistol

Gunpowder

ARMING THE TROOPS

During the 1500s, mounted soldiers began to use pistols in place of lances, bringing a new firepower to the battlefield. Wheel-lock pistols worked in all weathers and could be fired with one hand, unlike their clumsier predecessors, matchlocks. But they were expensive and not always reliable, and in the seventeenth century were replaced by the more efficient flintlock.

Ornate wheel-lock pistol

Embarkation of Henry VIII on board the *Henry Grâce-à-Dieu* in 1520

HENRY'S NAVY

Henry VIII was the first king to keep a permanent navy. Before him, monarchs relied on hiring ships from private owners when the need arose. There were just seven permanent ships in the English navy when Henry became king. Three years later, he had built that up to a fighting force of 18. Further ships were added, notably the *Henry Grâce-à-Dieu* (the *Great Harry*) and the *Mary Rose*, so that a fleet of 80 ships was available to fight the French navy in 1545.

Henry VIII's six wives

HENRY VIII's FIRST MARRIAGE was one of political convenience. It lasted 24 years, but produced only one child, a daughter. Henry took the unique step of having the marriage cancelled, or annulled, without the Pope's consent. His second marriage was a love match but it, too, failed to produce a son. This time he had his wife executed so he could replace her. His third wife died following the birth of the longed-for male heir. Two unhappy marriages followed. Only his sixth and final wife escaped either death or divorce.

THE ONLY SON
Henry was overjoyed when, on 12 October 1537, Jane Seymour gave birth to a son, Edward. Church bells were rung, celebration services were held throughout the land, and 2,000 guns were fired from the Tower of London.

Lettering decorated with gold leaf

Nativity scene

ANNE'S PRAYER BOOK
This Book of Hours, a bound collection of prayers and religious meditations, belonged to Anne Boleyn. Such books were painstakingly handwritten and illustrated by monks. It was given to Anne in 1522, and would probably have been her comfort before her execution.

ANOTHER DAUGHTER
Anne Boleyn's daughter Elizabeth, the future queen, was born on 7 September 1553. She was christened, wearing this robe, at Greenwich Palace on the River Thames. Henry was incensed at the birth of a second girl.

CATHERINE OF ARAGON
Henry's first wife Catherine of Aragon (1485–1536) was the daughter of the king and queen of Spain. She was originally married to Henry's older brother, Arthur, who died in 1502. The couple married in 1509 and, although she gave birth eight times, only one daughter, Mary, survived. Henry had his marriage to her annulled in 1533 – after he had secretly married his second wife.

ANNE BOLEYN
Henry fell in love with Anne Boleyn (c.1501–36), an aristocrat's daughter, in 1525. She refused to be just his mistress and the couple married in secret in 1532. After her failure to produce a son, Henry lost interest in her and, in 1536, she was executed on false charges of adultery.

JANE SEYMOUR
Henry's third wife Jane Seymour (c.1509–37) was one of Anne Boleyn's ladies-in-waiting. She married Henry just 11 days after Anne's execution. Tragically, she died only days after bearing Henry the son he had so craved.

The initial of Anne's surname

Beheading sword, made by a German craftsman

A SHARP, SWIFT INSTRUMENT
Two of Henry's wives, Anne Boleyn and Catherine Howard, were executed for treason. Because of their royal status, they were beheaded with a sword, not with the often blunt axe used for commoners.

> *"Even if I were to suffer a thousand deaths, my love for you would not abate one jot."*
>
> ANNE BOLEYN
> to Henry VIII

ANNE OF CLEVES
Henry agreed to marry his fourth wife Anne of Cleves (1515–57) after being shown this portrait of her. Anne was the daughter of a German prince, and their marriage was intended to strengthen England's ties with German states in the face of opposition from European Catholic powers. However, she evidently did not live up to her portrait – Henry called her the "Mare of Flanders" – and he divorced her in 1540, after just six months of marriage.

CATHERINE HOWARD
A cousin of Anne Boleyn, Catherine Howard (c.1525–42) married Henry just days after his divorce from Anne of Cleves. She was 19 and he 49. Henry called her his "rose without a thorn", but she was flirtatious and indiscrete, and he soon discovered a string of lovers. In 1542, she was executed for adultery.

CATHERINE PARR
Henry married his sixth and final wife Catherine Parr (c.1512–47) in 1543. Already twice widowed, she was known for her learning and sensitivity. Catherine proved an ideal stepmother for the three children, and she looked after Henry until he died in 1547.

IN THE TOWER
In Henry's time, the Tower of London was both a royal residence and a prison. Thus the first two of Henry's wives spent time here before their coronation as queen in Westminster Abbey. Both Anne Boleyn and Catherine Howard were held prisoner here before their execution on Tower Green inside its walls.

Traitors' Gate, through which important prisoners arrived

The break with Rome

HENRY'S DESIRE to rid himself of Catherine of Aragon so that he could remarry brought him into conflict with the Pope, the head of the Catholic Church in Rome. In 1533, Henry had his marriage annulled without papal consent. The Pope excommunicated him (excluded him from the Roman Catholic Church). In 1534, Henry retaliated by getting parliament to pass the Act of Supremacy, which established him as Supreme Head of the Church of England. While changes to religious doctrine followed the break with Rome, under Henry England continued to be a Catholic nation.

THE WEALTH OF THE CHURCH
The Church and the various monastic orders in England owned large estates and had, over the centuries, acquired huge wealth. As head of the Church of England, Henry could now claim these for the throne.

Sapphire

Gem-encrusted priest's chain

Nativity scene

AUTHORITY OF THE POPE
Although sovereign (answering to no-one but God) in their own land, all Christian monarchs in western Europe accepted the supreme authority of the Pope in Rome. It was this authority that Henry challenged after the Pope refused to annul his first marriage.

LUTHER AND HIS THESES
In 1517, German religious thinker, or theologian, Martin Luther published a list of 95 arguments, or theses, against corruption in the Catholic Church. This prompted a religious revolution across Europe known as the Reformation, which marked the emergence of the Protestant Church.

Legend has it that Luther nailed his theses to a church door

MONASTERIES DISSOLVED
By 1535, Henry VIII had taken on the role of Church reformer, which he realized had huge financial benefits for the Crown. He set up a commission to examine corruption in England's monasteries. Many of them were reported to be corrupt. By 1540, every monastery, abbey, friary, nunnery, and convent in the land had been closed, or dissolved. Their lands and other assets were taken over by the King.

The roof was removed for its valuable lead

Fountains Abbey, Yorkshire, dissolved in 1539

The burning of
Anne Askew

ANNE ASKEW
Influenced by the new European Protestant ideas, many women started to become active in religion and politics. One such was Anne Kyme, who left her husband, reverted to her maiden name of Askew and distributed Protestant pamphlets, including some, unwisely, to Catherine Parr, Henry's last wife. Askew was arrested, tortured on the rack, and then burned at the stake at Smithfield, London, in July 1546.

A monk teaching children before the dissolution of the monasteries

Illuminated initial letter (decorated, and with a picture inside it)

COMMUNITY WORK
The social impact of the dissolution of the monasteries was felt in every local community. Monks had once instructed children in Latin, theology, and other subjects, and given food and help to the poor and old. Without the monasteries, education suffered and rural poverty increased.

The Great Bible, 1539

SKILL OF THE MONKS
The dissolution of the monasteries caused a considerable amount of artistic desecration. Monks and nuns had developed a great skill for decorating manuscripts, mainly religious or devotional works such as this Book of Hours, as a way of contemplating the glory of God. These skills were lost after the monasteries closed, as were many of the manuscripts, which were either destroyed or sold into private hands.

DOING THE KING'S WORK
Thomas Cromwell (1485–1540) was one of the King's leading advisors. He used his administrative genius to organize the separation of the English Church from Rome. He also arranged the dissolution of the monasteries, transforming the royal finances, and reformed the workings of government. Cromwell was executed on a trumped-up charge of treason after the failure of the King's marriage to Anne of Cleves, which he had proposed.

THE BIBLE IN ENGLISH
Until the 1530s, all bibles in England were written in Latin. In 1537, Henry VIII furthered his break from Rome by authorizing an English translation to be read in churches. Two years later, a new translation by Miles Coverdale was issued as the Great Bible and became the authorized edition for use in churches until 1571.

The Reformation

EDWARD VI WAS ONLY NINE YEARS OLD when he succeeded his father Henry VIII to become king in 1547. Because he was a minor, the government was managed by a Protector. Under his guidance, and with the Protestant king's consent, the Archbishop of Canterbury was allowed to consolidate the Reformation begun under Henry. The old Catholic Church was swept away and a new Protestant Church set up, with services and prayer books in English. These changes led to unrest throughout the country, and revolts in Devon and Cornwall. The reforms were barely in place when Edward died, aged 15, in 1553.

THE PROTECTORS
As Edward was a minor, the government of the country was run by a Protector. At first, his uncle Edward Seymour, Duke of Somerset (above), took on the role. After 1550, control of government went to John Dudley, Duke of Northumberland.

PROTESTANT REFORMER
Archbishop of Canterbury Thomas Cranmer (1489–1556) was the religious thinker, or theologian, behind Henry VIII's break with Rome. Under Edward, he became an ardent Protestant and Church reformer. In 1549, he wrote the first Book of Common Prayer, replacing the Latin prose with English.

TUDOR SUCCESSION
This painting, a piece of Tudor propaganda, is intended to represent the triumph of the English Tudor monarchy against the Catholic Church. It shows the ailing Henry VIII passing on the succession to his son Edward, supported by his leading nobles and clerics. At their feet lies the defeated Pope, decorated with biblical quotations pointing out that all worldly power, including the Pope's own, comes to an end.

Henry VIII

Edward VI

Duke of Somerset, Lord Protector of England

Duke of Northumberland

Thomas Cranmer, Archbishop of Canterbury

St Mary Bethlehem hospital, London, re-established by Edward VI in 1547

NEW HOSPITALS
The dissolution of the monasteries under Henry VIII had closed many hospitals, as monks and nuns were the main providers of care for the sick. However, charity was central to Protestant ethics, and Edward supported the re-opening of many hospitals under state, or secular, ownership.

Stripping the churches

During the reign of Edward VI, the interiors of every church in the country were changed beyond all recognition. Between 1547 and 1553, almost all medieval English church art, statues and icons, prayer books, hymnals, and other books and manuscripts were destroyed. The Catholic mass became illegal. Two Acts of Uniformity, in 1549 and 1552, demanded that everyone accept the new Protestant religion.

Rosary with medals of saints

ROSARY BEADS
The rosary is the series of prayers recited by Catholics in a strict order, which they remember by counting out the prayers on a string of rosary beads. Thought to be empty ritualism or even idolatry by Protestants, the rosary was forbidden and the use of rosary beads outlawed.

ROOD SCREENS
In Catholic churches, an ornate carved screen with a crucifix, or rood, on top, separated the clergy at the altar from the congregation. Many of these screens were removed to emphasize the closer relationship of clergy and congregation in the new Church.

GOLD AND SILVER
In 1550, the clergy was instructed to eliminate all traces of idolatry ("idol-worship") from church services. Much valuable gold and silver ware, including chalices used to celebrate communion, was sold off or melted down, the proceeds going to the royal finances.

Jesus on the cross

Virgin Mary and baby Jesus

Heads of saints decorate the chalice

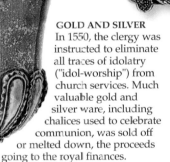

Plain whitewashed walls

REMOVING ICONS
As part of the removal of idolatry, or "idol-worship", statues and icons of the Virgin Mary and the saints were taken away from churches. The Protestants believed that they inhibited a direct relationship with God.

SIMPLE INTERIORS
Across England, every church and cathedral was stripped of its Catholic imagery. Statues were smashed, altars ripped out, chapels destroyed, and beautiful wall paintings whitewashed over to transform the once ornate interiors into bare places of worship.

Tudor childhood

IN TUDOR TIMES, childhood was often brutal and short-lived. It was commonly believed that physical punishment was an important part of bringing up children, both at home and at school. Privileged boys went to school, or were educated by tutors, learning subjects such as Latin, the universal language of the Church and law. Only the most high-born girls were educated. Adulthood came early. From the age of just seven, some children left home to become apprentices or servants in rich peoples' houses. Girls could be married at 12 and boys at 14.

The Lord's Prayer in Latin

A well-to-do Tudor schoolboy

HORNBOOK
Children learned to read from a hornbook, a sheet of paper fixed to a piece of wood and covered in transparent horn for protection. Texts such as the Lord's Prayer, which every pupil had to learn by heart, and verses from the Bible, were used as teaching aids.

Horn inkwells

Goose-feather quills

LEARNING TO WRITE
Writing was done with a quill pen, usually made from a goose feather. The feather was trimmed with a "penknife", and the tip cut at an angle to make the nib. Ink for the pen was stored in horn or pottery inkwells. Writing with a quill took a great deal of practice. Many of those who learned to read never learned to write as well.

BASIC EDUCATION
Infants received basic learning at "petty" or "dame" schools or, in some villages, at the local church hall. They were taught to read by the parish priest or a tutor, sometimes a woman. When they were six or seven, some richer boys went on to grammar schools. Poorer boys started learning a trade.

Pupils line up to recite their Latin grammar, hoping to avoid a thrashing

KEEPING ORDER IN THE CLASSROOM
Beatings were part of the Tudor theory of education, and students were regularly whipped with canes, bundles of birch twigs, or leather straps. Although most teachers and educational theorists believed that pain was good for the soul, there were exceptions, such as the scholar Erasmus, who advocated humane treatment in his book *On The Teaching of Boys*.

Names of old students inscribed on beams

A PROFESSIONAL TRAINING
The Royal Grammar School in Guildford, Surrey, was founded by Edward VI, and is still in use today. In Tudor times, grammar schools combined classical subjects, such as Latin grammar (essential for boys who planned to have a profession), logic, and rhetoric (the effective use of speech), with practical skills such as writing and arithmetic.

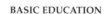

THOMAS BAKER. MAIOR 1565.

HIGHER EDUCATION

University education was available for bright grammar school boys at either Oxford or Cambridge, the only two universities then in existence. There they could study divinity, civil law, physic (medicine), Hebrew, and Greek. It was common to start university as young as 14, although Thomas Wolsey, who became cardinal of England under Henry VIII, began at Oxford when he was only 11.

Christ Church College, Oxford, founded 1546

Tudor rocking horse

CHILD LABOUR

Children are among the workers at this 16th-century printing press

At the age of seven to nine, many poorer children, mostly boys, left home to become apprenticed to a skilled craftsman. Tied to the master by a strict oath, and provided with a place to stay, food to eat, and the necessary clothes and tools, the apprentice assisted his master at work, gradually picking up the trade.

TUDOR TOYS

The nurseries of richer children were filled with rocking horses, wooden toys and games, and dolls. Tiny cups and saucers made of tin and lead and model ships and castles were displayed there, in purpose-built cabinets. Poorer children made their own toys out of scraps of wood lying about the farm or street.

PLAYTIME

Out in the street, children made up their own games and entertainments, spinning wooden hoops, playing leapfrog and catch, bowls, and the then extremely violent game of football. No playgrounds were provided for children, so their games took place in crowded streets or in the few available large squares and courtyards.

Playing leapfrog

Spinning a hoop

Three Sisters by an unknown 16th-century artist

Children wore fine jewellery if their parents could afford it

TINY ADULTS

Tudor babies were dressed in swaddling clothes – layers of tightly wrapped cotton. This was thought to make their limbs grow straight. Once out of babyhood, children wore miniature versions of their parents' clothes. They were expected to behave formally too, even with their own families. When their parents entered the room, boys took their caps off and girls had to curtsey.

Bloody Mary

IN 1533, when she was 17, Mary's father Henry VIII had his marriage to her mother Catherine of Aragon annulled and declared Mary illegitimate. When her brother Edward was king, he tried to make sure the Protestant Lady Jane Grey inherited the throne after his death, but the country rose up in favour of Mary as the legitimate heir. She became queen in 1553, the first English female monarch since the 1100s. She restored Catholicism as the state religion and began a fierce campaign against those she saw as enemies of God – Protestants. Her short reign is chiefly remembered for the burnings of 300 Protestants, which gained her the name "Bloody Mary", and for her alliance with Spain, the leading Catholic state in Europe, whose heir to the throne she married.

CATHOLIC REVIVAL
Under Mary, papal supremacy (the Pope's authority) was reintroduced. Mass was celebrated once again, Catholic bishops and clerics replaced Protestant ones, and all the Protestant legislation of the past decades was repealed.

Ornate Catholic cross

A TROUBLED LIFE
Mary was a devout Catholic and, while her strong beliefs gave her great certainty, they also made her merciless towards Protestants. She was personally responsible for much of the religious persecution during her reign. Mary wanted desperately to have a child to prevent her Protestant sister Elizabeth succeeding to the throne. But she died childless, probably of cancer, aged 42.

QUEEN FOR NINE DAYS
As Edward VI lay dying, he nominated Lady Jane Grey, the Protestant granddaughter of Henry VIII's sister, Mary, as his heir. When Edward died on 6 July 1553, Jane was proclaimed queen. Nine days later, Mary marched on London with her supporters and took her rightful throne. Lady Jane Grey was beheaded in 1554.

The apostle Mark

CRANMER'S DEATH

The most famous Protestant martyr was Archbishop Cranmer, who had engineered Henry VIII's divorce from Mary's mother. He was also implicated in the plot to place Lady Jane Grey on the throne. In 1556, he was burned at the stake for heresy – having the wrong religious beliefs.

BOOK OF MARTYRS

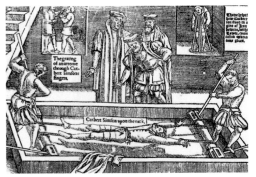

After Mary's death, Protestant writer John Foxe compiled a *Book of Martyrs*, with accounts of all those who had been burnt or punished for their beliefs. A copy was put in every church to remind people of Mary's cruel reign. Here, a Protestant is tortured on the rack.

LOSS OF CALAIS

English kings had controlled territory in France since the Norman invasion of England in 1066. By Mary's reign, the only possession left was the port of Calais, which had been English since 1347. In 1557, England and Spain declared war against France, Spain's main enemy in Europe. The French besieged Calais and easily captured the town. Its loss was a national humiliation, and Mary took it as a personal failure.

Luke, one of the four apostles whose images decorate the cross

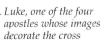

Calais with its protecting sea wall

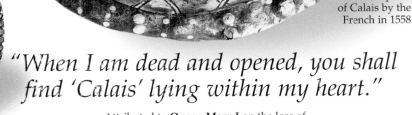

Enamel plaque showing the capture of Calais by the French in 1558

TUDOR SATIRE

Stephen Gardiner (1497–1555), Bishop of Winchester under Henry, became Lord Chancellor under Mary. This anti-Catholic painting shows him eating animal flesh in a probable satire of the Catholic mass, in which a wafer is believed to convert to the body of Christ. It may have been painted abroad, away from Mary's reach.

PHILIP OF SPAIN

Mary's marriage to Philip, heir to the Spanish throne, was hugely unpopular. Many people disliked the idea of a Catholic foreigner sharing the throne, and Spain was considered an enemy. The marriage was not a success. When Philip became king of Spain in 1556, he left England for good, two years before Mary's death.

"When I am dead and opened, you shall find 'Calais' lying within my heart."

Attributed to **Queen Mary I** on the loss of England's only continental possession

The young Elizabeth

SUSPICIOUS SISTER
In 1554, Elizabeth was imprisoned by her sister Mary I in the Tower of London on suspicion of treason. Mary believed Elizabeth had been involved in the short-lived Wyatt rebellion against her rule, although no actual evidence existed. She was released after three months, but spent the next year under house arrest in Woodstock, Oxfordshire.

ELIZABETH BECAME QUEEN after the death of her sister Mary I in 1558. She was 25. She had had a difficult path to the throne and, once there, her position was by no means secure. Many Catholics did not believe Elizabeth should be queen because she had been declared illegitimate as a child. Tension between Catholics and Protestants was also a major problem. With the aid of clever, capable advisors, and using her own political skill, she was able to instate a benign form of Protestantism. This succeeded in both containing the unrest and securing her own position.

Elizabeth in her coronation robes

Royal sceptre, symbol of sovereignty

RING OF AFFECTION
Elizabeth hardly knew her mother Anne Boleyn, who was disgraced and executed for treason when Elizabeth was only three years old. One of the few reminders of her mother was this diamond, ruby, and pearl-encrusted locket ring, with her mother's portrait facing her own.

Anne Boleyn, Elizabeth's dead mother

Elizabeth

CHILDHOOD HOME
Elizabeth spent much of her childhood at Hatfield House in Hertfordshire and it was her main home from 1555–58. It was here, on 17 November 1558, while sitting under an oak tree, that she heard the news of her sister's death. Overcome at the thought that she was to be queen, she fell on her knees and, quoting Psalm 118, said, "This is the Lord's doing; it is marvellous in our eyes."

Mother-of-pearl locket ring opens to reveal family portraits

Orpharian player

16th-century opharian

12 wire strings

Inset pearls

SCHOLAR AND MUSICIAN
Like her sister Mary, Elizabeth was a fine linguist, reading Latin and Greek fluently as well as speaking many European languages. She was also an accomplished poet. She enjoyed dancing and hunting, and was a skilled musician. This ornate orphorion was once owned by Elizabeth. She also played the lute and keyboards, sometimes alone to "shun melancholy", but also to entertain an audience at court.

Decorative walnut inlay

Royal footmen

Elizabeth's coronation procession

THE CORONATION
On Saturday 15 January 1559, Elizabeth processed through the streets of London from the Tower to the palace of Whitehall. Crowds lined the streets, which were decorated with banners and streamers. Along the way, players and musicians performed in her honour on specially built stages. The next day, she walked along the newly gravelled streets, which were covered with blue cloth, to be crowned queen in Westminster Abbey.

CHARACTER OF A QUEEN
Unlike her brother and sister, Elizabeth had inherited her father's red hair and fair skin, and much of his charisma. Her strong personality always made her the centre of attention. She was intelligent, shrewd, and tolerant, but could also be vain, impetuous, and very sarcastic.

Orb, a symbol of royal power and justice

FAITHFUL ADVISOR
William Cecil (1520–98), served Elizabeth loyally for 40 years as Secretary and Lord Treasurer. One of his tasks was to represent royal policy to Parliament. Cecil worked tirelessly to protect Elizabeth's interests and support her authority.

A MODERATE ARCHBISHOP
The man most responsible for the return to Protestantism under Elizabeth was Matthew Parker (1504–75), Archbishop of Canterbury from 1559. His great success was in upholding a moderate form of Protestantism. Also a wise and learned scholar, Parker sponsored many works of history, and helped to preserve medieval manuscripts.

Triptych of the Royal Arms from the Church of St Mary's, Suffolk

ELIZABETHA MAGNA · REGINA ANGLIÆ

ELIZABETHAN RELIGION
Under Elizabeth, the Protestant religion of Edward VI was reinstated in less extreme form, after the brief Catholic period under Mary. Elizabeth was made Supreme Governor of the Church and the royal coat of arms was hung on the wall in most churches, sometimes in the form of a triptych, or three-panelled painting. Elizabeth was not as zealous in her religion as her brother and sister. Unlike them, she held back from a vigorous persecution of religious difference.

Tudor costume

IN TUDOR TIMES, as today, clothes were a symbol of class and wealth. Unlike today, however, there were strict regulations in force stating what could and could not be worn. These Sumptuary Laws, as they were called, enforced the wearing of English-made cloth in an attempt to bolster the home textile industry. Also, they were intended to maintain distinctions between the social classes by confining the wearing of finer fabrics to the nobility. During Mary I's reign, for example, only those who had been knighted were permitted to wear silk.

French hood, made popular by Anne Boleyn

Gown, worn fashionably over the shoulder

Men were clean-shaven in early Tudor times

Gold, emerald, and diamond hat jewel

Richly patterned doublet

THE FIRE JEWEL
Tudor hat jewels were often symbolic as well as decorative. The salamander was wrongly believed to be able to survive fire, so this jewel was worn to suggest strength and vigour.

Close-fitting tights, or hose, attached to the doublet by laces

EARLY TUDOR MAN
Men wore a shirt of wool, linen, or sometimes silk. Over this they wore a close-fitting jacket, or doublet, made of wool or a canvas and wool mix known as kersey. A working man wore a woollen jerkin or jacket, while a rich man wore a short-sleeved robe or gown. Wealthy men's clothes were often made from heavy, elaborately patterned fabrics.

EARLY TUDOR WOMAN
At the start of the Tudor period, well-dressed women wore heavy, floor-length gowns of velvet or silk. These had low, square-cut necklines often decorated with jewels, and embroidered panels on the bodice – the part from neck to waist. Women's hair was swept back from their faces and kept tidy under a French hood.

Cotton underskirt beneath velvet gown

ELIZABETHAN MAN
After about 1540, a major change in fashion occurred. Men stopped wearing hose and replaced them with a padded, round trunk below the waist, breeches (or canions) down to the knee, and stockings underneath. The doublet was padded both at the shoulders and at the hips. This had the effect of making a man look broader at the shoulders and narrower at the waist.

Starched linen ruff

Jewelled band to keep hair off face

Ruffs around the wrists match the neck ruff

WOOLLEN CAP
In 1571, a Sumptuary Law was passed ordering everybody over the age of six and below a certain rank to wear a woollen cap on Sundays and holidays. The English wool industry received a boost as a result.

Padded, decorated trunk

Velvet breeches, or canions

FASHION SENSE
The fashion for wide shoes became so pronounced in Tudor times that, under Henry VIII, a statute was passed limiting their width to 15 cm (6 in). Square-ended shoes, like this 500-year-old example, were low-cut and flat.

Gable hood with padded band decorated with jewels

FASHIONABLE HEADDRESS
The gable hood was made popular in England by Henry VIII's first wife, Catherine of Aragon. Made of rich fabric such as velvet or damask, it was worn over a tight-fitting undercap and reached half-way down the back. It lost popularity while Anne Boleyn was queen, as she favoured the French hood.

Cinnabar used for red blusher

MIXING MAKE-UP
The bright-red mineral cinnabar was used as a blusher, and tin made the cheeks white. Make-up was prepared by mixing minerals such as talc with fig juice and other liquids and grinding them to a paste in a pestle and mortar.

Talc

Pestle and mortar

Fig

Tin

ELIZABETHAN WOMAN
Wide dresses padded out over wire, cane, or whalebone frames were worn by Elizabethan women to emphasize narrow waists. Necklines stayed square-cut and low, with a frill collar worn around the neck, and shoulders were padded and frilled. If her hair was grey, the lady wore a wig, decorated with jewels.

STATELY GLOVES
Noble women wore ornate, perfumed gloves. This pair was given to Elizabeth I when she visited the University of Oxford in 1566. Gloves were a safe present to give the Queen, as she was proud of her shapely hands.

Elizabeth's golden age

ELIZABETH WAS ONE OF the most successful monarchs ever to sit on the English throne. Her reign, during which England became an important European power and art and culture flourished, is often called a "golden age". Female leaders were – and still are – rare enough, but it was unheard of for one to remain single. But Elizabeth would not share the throne. She liked to say that she was "married to England". Throughout her reign, Elizabeth retained her popularity through skillful manipulation of public opinion – making clever speeches and directing the way she was portrayed by artists.

Egg white

Poppy seeds

PRESENTING A FACE
As she aged, Elizabeth was careful to appear as young as possible in public. She wore elaborate make-up to cover her smallpox scars. (The public was led to believe that she had been unmarked by the disease, but this was not true.) But the lead and mercury base of most cosmetics then used were toxic, and probably contributed to the deterioration of her skin.

Elizabeth wore a full wig to conceal her grey hair

Pelican's bloody chest, a symbol of sacrifice

A MOTHER'S LOVE
Female pelicans were wrongly thought to feed their young on flesh plucked from their own chests. Elizabeth wore this brooch as a symbol of the self-sacrificing, motherly care she lavished on her subjects.

REPRESENTING THE QUEEN
Hundreds of paintings of Elizabeth were made during her lifetime, but few were done directly from life. One painting served as a template for other artists. Since few of her subjects would ever see Elizabeth in the flesh, her portraits did not have to be too realistic. Instead, they were painted to show her as a symbol of her nation's strength and ambitions.

Pearls symbolized chastity

SMALLPOX
In 1562, Elizabeth caught smallpox, a disease that almost killed her. This medal was struck to commemorate her recovery. The image alludes to St Paul being bitten by a snake – an incident that left him unharmed, implying that the queen too was unscathed.

Globe, a symbol of imperial domination

Ingredients of typical Elizabethan make-up

Borax

Mercury

Lead

ROBERT DEVEREUX
Robert Devereux's good looks brought him to the attention of the queen in the late 1580s. However, in 1600, he was placed under house arrest after he disobeyed her orders while attempting to put down a rebellion in Ireland. Faced with financial and political ruin, he attempted to overthrow the government and, in 1601, was tried and executed for treason.

Robert Devereux, 2nd Earl of Essex

Robert Dudley, 1st Earl of Leicester

ROBERT DUDLEY
Had she married, Elizabeth's first choice of husband would probably have been the dashing Robert Dudley, whom she had known since childhood. However, he was considered unsuitable because his first wife Amy had died in suspicious circumstances. Also, many people felt that it would be wrong for Elizabeth to marry one of her own subjects, rather than a foreign monarch. But she remained closely attached to him until his death in 1588.

ADDRESSING THE TROOPS
Elizabeth knew the impact a few stirring words could have. She was a skilled orator and wrote all her own speeches. When the Spanish Armada threatened England in 1588, the Earl of Leicester, commander of the English army, suggested she rally the troops herself. On 9 August she addressed them at Tilbury, Essex. Her speech started with the famous words: "I know I have the body of a weak and feeble woman, but I have the heart and stomach of a king, and of a king of England too."

ROYAL GIFTS
Every New Year, Elizabeth exchanged gifts with her courtiers and servants. The more important courtiers were given gold plated items, and the lower ranks clothes or accessories. Elizabeth supposedly gave these mittens to Margaret Edgecumbe, a maid of honour, in about 1600.

Silk embroidery in pattern of foliage, a popular 16th-century design

Carved, gilded mahogany

A FEMALE SKILL
This mahogany chair, one of a pair, is said to have been embroidered by the Queen and given to Elizabeth More, one of her ladies-in-waiting. Whether true or not, the Queen was certainly an expert needleworker, a skill she learned as a child and which she kept up throughout her life.

Ornate low chair

Trade and exploration

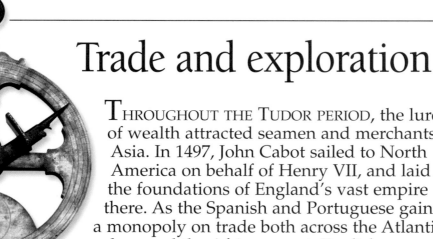

THROUGHOUT THE TUDOR PERIOD, the lure of wealth attracted seamen and merchants to Asia. In 1497, John Cabot sailed to North America on behalf of Henry VII, and laid the foundations of England's vast empire there. As the Spanish and Portuguese gained a monopoly on trade both across the Atlantic and around the African coast, English seamen searched north for new routes to Asia. Unfortunately, they proved unsuccessful. A more lucrative venture was piracy. Encouraged by Queen Elizabeth I, Drake and other seamen regularly plundered Spanish ships carrying valuables home, bringing great wealth into England.

Crew keep watch for land from crow's-nest

HOW FAR WEST?
Navigation was not an exact science. Sailors had a compass to indicate direction and an astrolabe (above) to measure the height of the Sun at noon in order to determine how far north or south they were. But, crucially, they had no way of determining how far east or west they were.

Drake's ships raiding Santo Domingo in the Caribbean

RAIDING THE SPANISH
The man who did the most to establish England as a maritime threat to Spain was Francis Drake (1542–96). In 1577–81, he became the first Englishman to circumnavigate the globe. During that voyage, he raided several Spanish settlements and returned to England a rich man. Later, supported by Elizabeth I, he raided Spanish ships and settlements in the Caribbean. In his 1588 attack on Santo Domingo, Drake's men completely destroyed the town.

LOOKING FOR CHINA
Italian navigator John Cabot (Giovanni Caboto) (c.1450–1499) set out to prove that the quickest route to China was across the North Atlantic. Spanish and Portuguese kings refused to finance him but, in 1497, he sailed from Bristol with the support of Henry VII. Instead of finding China, as he thought he would, Cabot discovered Newfoundland (or possibly Nova Scotia), which he claimed for England.

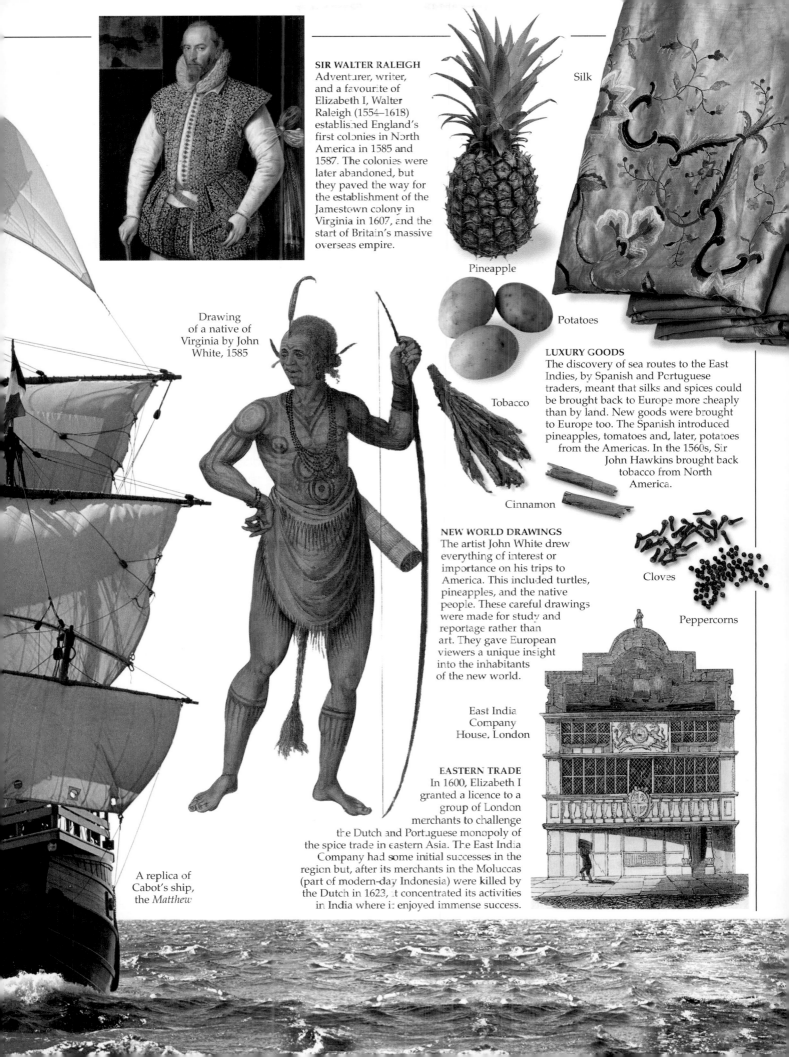

SIR WALTER RALEIGH
Adventurer, writer, and a favourite of Elizabeth I, Walter Raleigh (1554–1618) established England's first colonies in North America in 1585 and 1587. The colonies were later abandoned, but they paved the way for the establishment of the Jamestown colony in Virginia in 1607, and the start of Britain's massive overseas empire.

Silk

Pineapple

Potatoes

Drawing of a native of Virginia by John White, 1585

Tobacco

Cinnamon

LUXURY GOODS
The discovery of sea routes to the East Indies, by Spanish and Portuguese traders, meant that silks and spices could be brought back to Europe more cheaply than by land. New goods were brought to Europe too. The Spanish introduced pineapples, tomatoes and, later, potatoes from the Americas. In the 1560s, Sir John Hawkins brought back tobacco from North America.

NEW WORLD DRAWINGS
The artist John White drew everything of interest or importance on his trips to America. This included turtles, pineapples, and the native people. These careful drawings were made for study and reportage rather than art. They gave European viewers a unique insight into the inhabitants of the new world.

Cloves

Peppercorns

East India Company House, London

EASTERN TRADE
In 1600, Elizabeth I granted a licence to a group of London merchants to challenge the Dutch and Portuguese monopoly of the spice trade in eastern Asia. The East India Company had some initial successes in the region but, after its merchants in the Moluccas (part of modern-day Indonesia) were killed by the Dutch in 1623, it concentrated its activities in India where it enjoyed immense success.

A replica of Cabot's ship, the *Matthew*

Mary Queen of Scots

ENGLAND AND SCOTLAND had been uneasy neighbours for centuries, their distrust of each other often erupting into open warfare. Relations between the two countries took a surprising turn of events in 1567, however. The Scottish queen, Mary, was forced to abdicate as a result of her scandalous personal life, and she fled for safety to England. Catholic Mary presented a real threat to her cousin Queen Elizabeth, as some would have liked to see her on the English throne, and she was held captive for 20 years. When Mary foolishly plotted to assassinate Elizabeth, she was tried for treason and executed.

A FRENCH CHILDHOOD
In 1548, the five-year-old Mary was sent to France. She may have lived here at Chenonceau. In 1558, she married the heir, or dauphin, to the French throne, who soon became king as Francis II. His reign was short, however, and in 1560 Mary was widowed, aged just 18. She returned to Scotland in 1561, almost a stranger in her own land.

The dauphin Francis

SCANDALOUS LOVE LIFE
Mary had a considerable intellect, but she was also hot-tempered and headstrong. By the age of 25, she had been married three times and twice widowed. Furthermore, her third husband, the Earl of Bothwell, had been divorced just 12 days when he married Mary, and was strongly suspected of murdering Mary's previous husband. All this was too much for Mary's subjects, who turned against her, forcing her to abdicate.

Mary dancing with Lord Darnley

LORD DARNLEY
Mary's second husband was her cousin, Lord Darnley, an English nobleman. They had a son, who became James VI of Scotland (and, after the death of Elizabeth, king of England). But, within months of the marriage, Darnley had become irrationally jealous of Mary's secretary, David Rizzio. Together with some accomplices, he murdered Rizzio in front of Mary. Months later, Darnley himself was murdered.

BABY QUEEN
Mary was born on 8 December 1542 in Linlithgow, the royal palace of Scottish kings. Six days later her father, James V, died. Mary was crowned queen of Scotland when she was nine months old, a title she lost, aged 27, in 1567.

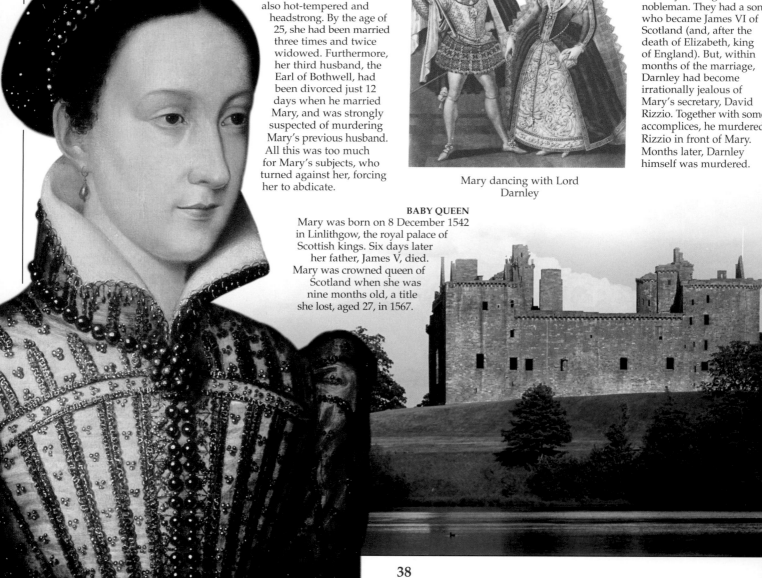

CATHOLIC THREAT

Mary sought refuge in England, but Elizabeth could not allow her to live freely there. Many Catholics saw Elizabeth as the illegitimate daughter of Henry VIII and his mistress, and thus without a true right to the crown. As a legitimate descendant of Henry VIII's older sister Margaret, they believed Mary to be the true heir to the English throne.

Mary's own prayer book and rosary beads

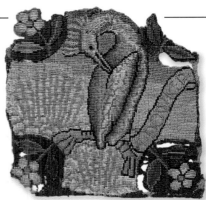

STITCHING TIME

Mary spent 20 years in prison in England. She filled her time with embroidery, as well as reading and letter writing. Along with two friends, she embroidered the beautiful Oxburgh Hanging, a detail of which is shown here.

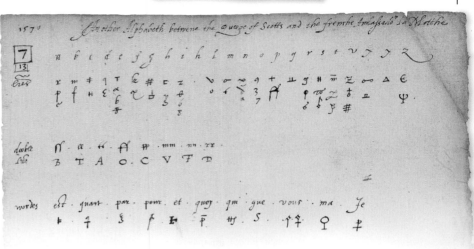

ELIZABETH'S SPYMASTER

As principal royal secretary from 1573, Sir Francis Walsingham maintained a network of agents to spy on Elizabeth's enemies, and he uncovered many plots against her. In 1586, he successfully infiltrated the plot by the Catholic Anthony Babington to assassinate Elizabeth. Mary was one of those implicated in its planning. Walsingham's evidence was enough to convict her of treason.

SECRET CODE

Whilst in prison, Mary kept her correspondence secret by writing her letters in code, using 23 symbols for letters of the alphabet and a further 36 for whole words. However, all her letters were intercepted by Walsingham and decoded by the master codebreaker, Thomas Phelippes, who used the code to set a trap to discover who the Babington conspirators were.

Warrant to Execute Mary Stuart

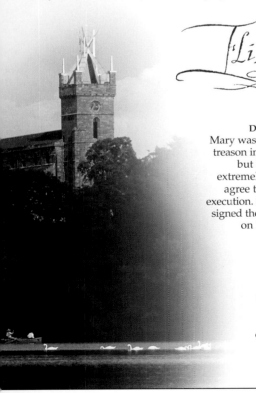

DEATH WARRANT

Mary was found guilty of treason in October 1586, but Elizabeth was extremely reluctant to agree to her cousin's execution. She eventually signed the death warrant on 1 February 1587.

THE EXECUTION

Mary was beheaded at Fotheringhay Castle, Northamptonshire, on 8 February 1587, observed by about 300 people. Her death shocked her son, by now James VI of Scotland, and appalled Catholic Europe. It also provided Phillip II of Spain with added justification for the Armada he was about to launch to invade England.

The Spanish Armada

PLAYING FOR TIME
In April 1587, Sir Francis Drake (above) set back Spain's invasion plans by more than a year when he raided their fleet at anchor in Cadiz, Spain, destroying 37 ships. This gave the English vital time to prepare. He later commanded one of the four fleets that defeated the Armada itself.

Wheel-mounted cannon

In 1588, England faced its biggest danger for centuries. A huge Spanish fleet, the Armada, had set sail to ferry an invasion army across from the Netherlands. Relations between Protestant England and Catholic Spain had been poor for some years. England's support of Dutch rebels fighting for independence from Spain, and the execution of the Catholic Mary Queen of Scots, worsened them further. Philip II of Spain was determined to invade the country and overthrow Elizabeth. The English, however, were ready. A combination of superior seamanship, artillery tactics, and bad weather saw the Armada off, and the threat was lifted.

BATTLE TACTICS
Both Spanish and English fleets carried similar types of cannon, but the two sides deployed them in different ways. The Spanish used guns at close range to stop an enemy ship before coming alongside and boarding it. The English used theirs to attack the hull and rigging with repeated fire to damage or even sink the ship. This approach was made possible by the invention, during Henry VIII's reign, of a mobile, four-wheeled gun-carriage, which made it easier to fire, pull back, reload, and then fire the cannon again in quick succession.

Cannon balls

The Armada, 1590s, English school

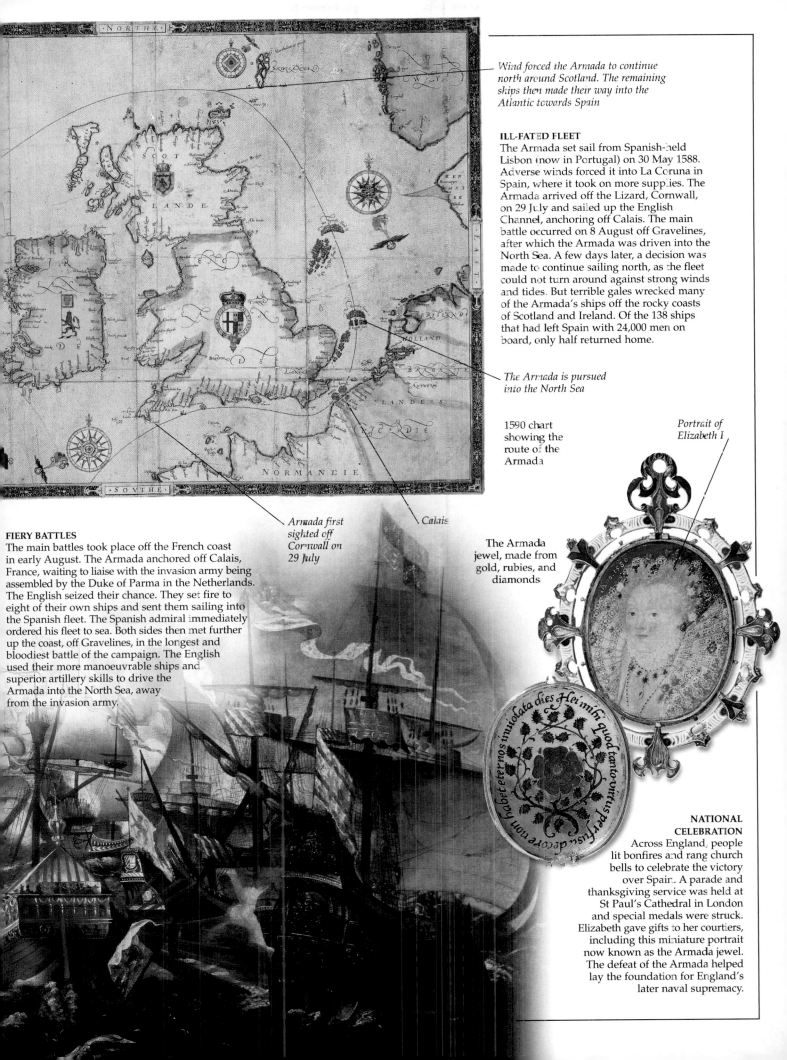

Wind forced the Armada to continue north around Scotland. The remaining ships then made their way into the Atlantic towards Spain

ILL-FATED FLEET

The Armada set sail from Spanish-held Lisbon (now in Portugal) on 30 May 1588. Adverse winds forced it into La Coruna in Spain, where it took on more supplies. The Armada arrived off the Lizard, Cornwall, on 29 July and sailed up the English Channel, anchoring off Calais. The main battle occurred on 8 August off Gravelines, after which the Armada was driven into the North Sea. A few days later, a decision was made to continue sailing north, as the fleet could not turn around against strong winds and tides. But terrible gales wrecked many of the Armada's ships off the rocky coasts of Scotland and Ireland. Of the 138 ships that had left Spain with 24,000 men on board, only half returned home.

The Armada is pursued into the North Sea

1590 chart showing the route of the Armada

Portrait of Elizabeth I

The Armada jewel, made from gold, rubies, and diamonds

Armada first sighted off Cornwall on 29 July

Calais

FIERY BATTLES

The main battles took place off the French coast in early August. The Armada anchored off Calais, France, waiting to liaise with the invasion army being assembled by the Duke of Parma in the Netherlands. The English seized their chance. They set fire to eight of their own ships and sent them sailing into the Spanish fleet. The Spanish admiral immediately ordered his fleet to sea. Both sides then met further up the coast, off Gravelines, in the longest and bloodiest battle of the campaign. The English used their more manoeuvrable ships and superior artillery skills to drive the Armada into the North Sea, away from the invasion army.

NATIONAL CELEBRATION

Across England, people lit bonfires and rang church bells to celebrate the victory over Spain. A parade and thanksgiving service was held at St Paul's Cathedral in London and special medals were struck. Elizabeth gave gifts to her courtiers, including this miniature portrait now known as the Armada jewel. The defeat of the Armada helped lay the foundation for England's later naval supremacy.

Tudor London

A<small>T THE HEART</small> of Tudor England was the capital city, London, by far the biggest city in the country and one of the largest in Europe. Between 1500 and 1600, the population grew from just 50,000 to about 200,000. London sat either side of the River Thames, a busy waterway filled with ferries and boats bringing in goods from the ports of northern Europe. The city was the administrative and political capital of England as well as its trading and commercial centre. Its bustling warren of streets were packed with merchants, shopkeepers, craftsmen, street sellers, travelling players, and pickpockets.

St Paul's cathedral

Globe theatre

View of London from the south by Claes Jans Visscher, c.1616

Waterman

LONDON'S LAYOUT
The historic centre of the Tudor capital was enclosed by two-and-a-half miles of walls, originally built by the Romans. But London had already spread beyond these city walls. The royal palace of Whitehall and Westminster, home of parliament, lay to its west. South of the Thames was Southwark, connected to the centre by London Bridge, the only river crossing between the sea and the bridge at Kingston, 20 miles upstream.

WATERBORNE
As London Bridge was the only river crossing, more than 2,000 wherries – long, light rowing-boats – worked on the Thames. Watermen waited at quays to pick up passengers and row them up and down the river or across to the other bank for a few pennies.

London Bridge, where traitors' heads were displayed on poles

TOWER OF LONDON
Downstream from London Bridge on the north bank of the Thames, the Tower of London guarded the city. While both Henry VII and his son extended and refurbished the royal quarters inside its walls, the main use of the Tower during Tudor times was as a state prison.

Lanterns, as used by Tudor nightwatchmen

CURFEW AT DUSK
Every evening at dusk, church bells rang to announce the curfew. The city gates were closed, the taverns and shops were shut, and everyone went home. After dark, nightwatchmen patrolled the streets with lanterns to deter criminals.

RUNNING LONDON
The Lord Mayor was the elected head of the city of London, responsible for governing the city and administering justice. Most of the day-to-day work in running London was carried out by the Court of Common Council, whose members were elected annually by London's citizens.

TUDOR FOOD TO GO
Street sellers sold their produce from baskets or panniers strapped to a donkey or small horse. Fresh fish and seafood, seasonal fruit and vegetables, sausages and other meats, hot pies, baked apples and a wide range of pastries could all be bought from the sellers, whose personal cries advertising their wares were a distinctive sound in Tudor London.

TUDOR SHOPPING
In Tudor London, traders or craftsmen selling similar goods sometimes had shops in the same street. Tailors, for instance, could be found in Threadneedle Street, and shoemakers in Shoe Lane. Each shop had a painted sign hanging outside to distinguish one from another.

Upper stories jut out into the street to increase space inside the house

STREET LIFE
Pickpockets, or cutpurses as they were known, were numerous in Tudor London. They used a knife to cut the strings that tied a purse to its owner's belt, a practice known as "nipping a bung". Some were trained at an illegal "school" near Billingsgate Market, run by "Wotton, a gentleman born and [formerly] a merchant of good credit".

TUDOR BUILDING
London's houses and shops were mostly built of clay brick or wood, as both were readily available locally. The winding narrow streets made it difficult to manoeuvre long wooden beams, so big buildings were prefabricated out of London and brought along the river for assembly on site. A few were constructed of stone removed from the recently closed monasteries and friaries.

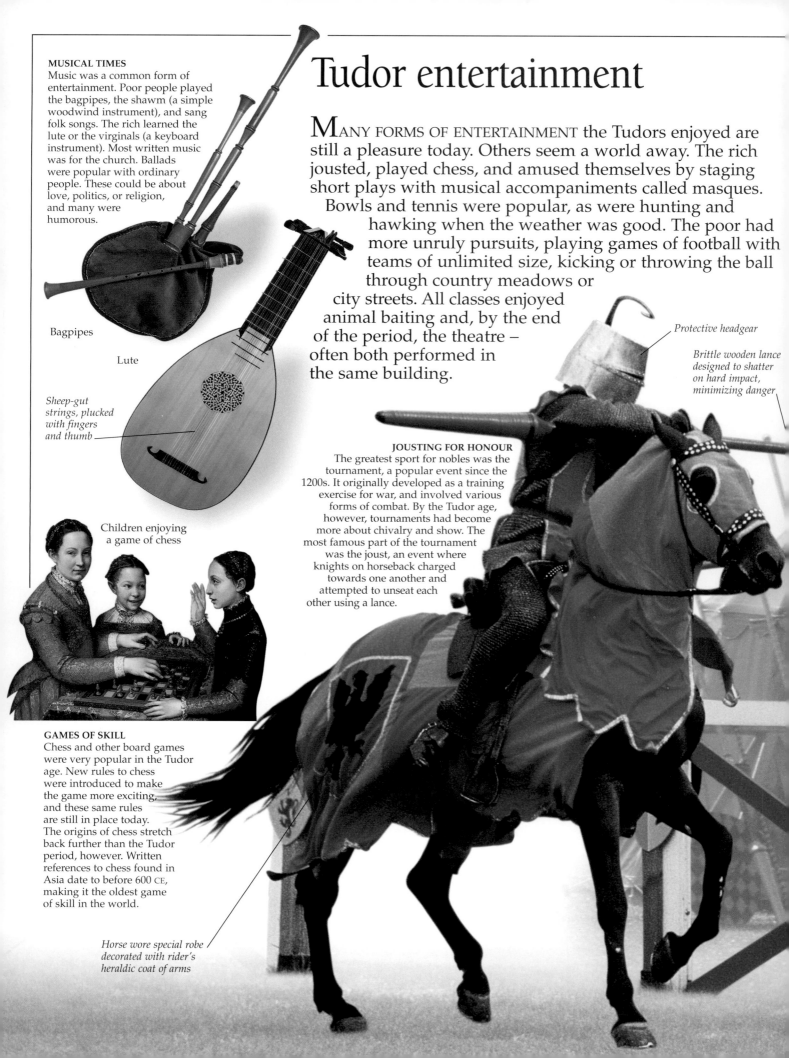

Tudor entertainment

MANY FORMS OF ENTERTAINMENT the Tudors enjoyed are still a pleasure today. Others seem a world away. The rich jousted, played chess, and amused themselves by staging short plays with musical accompaniments called masques. Bowls and tennis were popular, as were hunting and hawking when the weather was good. The poor had more unruly pursuits, playing games of football with teams of unlimited size, kicking or throwing the ball through country meadows or city streets. All classes enjoyed animal baiting and, by the end of the period, the theatre – often both performed in the same building.

MUSICAL TIMES
Music was a common form of entertainment. Poor people played the bagpipes, the shawm (a simple woodwind instrument), and sang folk songs. The rich learned the lute or the virginals (a keyboard instrument). Most written music was for the church. Ballads were popular with ordinary people. These could be about love, politics, or religion, and many were humorous.

Bagpipes

Lute

Sheep-gut strings, plucked with fingers and thumb

Children enjoying a game of chess

GAMES OF SKILL
Chess and other board games were very popular in the Tudor age. New rules to chess were introduced to make the game more exciting, and these same rules are still in place today. The origins of chess stretch back further than the Tudor period, however. Written references to chess found in Asia date to before 600 CE, making it the oldest game of skill in the world.

Horse wore special robe decorated with rider's heraldic coat of arms

JOUSTING FOR HONOUR
The greatest sport for nobles was the tournament, a popular event since the 1200s. It originally developed as a training exercise for war, and involved various forms of combat. By the Tudor age, however, tournaments had become more about chivalry and show. The most famous part of the tournament was the joust, an event where knights on horseback charged towards one another and attempted to unseat each other using a lance.

Protective headgear

Brittle wooden lance designed to shatter on hard impact, minimizing danger

REAL TENNIS

Tennis was so associated with the monarchy that when lawn tennis began in the 19th century, the original indoor game became known as real or royal tennis to distinguish between the two. It was played using leather balls stuffed with human hair. Poor women would sell their hair for the balls as a source of income.

A DOG'S CHANCE

The cruel sport of bear-baiting was popular with all classes. Monarchs and nobles kept their own bears, while poorer people went to public bear-baits. The bear was tied to a post and attacked by dogs, which tried to tear its throat out. The bear's teeth were sometimes removed, so it could defend itself only with its paws.

THE THEATRE

Travelling players performing plays and reciting verse in the streets were a familiar sight in market towns, but purpose-built theatres were found only in London. At the start of the Tudor age, most performances were of morality plays dealing with human vice and religious virtue. By the end of Elizabeth's reign, William Shakespeare (p.47) and Christopher Marlowe were writing plays that are still performed today.

A performance of Shakespeare's *Hamlet*

Cocks fighting, using their beaks and feet

COCKFIGHTING

Watching a pair of cockerels fight each other to the death was common entertainment. At the cockpit near Smithfield in London, spectators paid one penny to watch the contest from the gallery, while those who wanted to bet on the result paid more to sit at a ring-side seat.

Heraldic coat of arms

Competitors separated by wooden rail

The end of an era

THE DEATH OF ELIZABETH I in 1603 marked the end not just of a reign but of an era too. Elizabeth had no children, so the Tudor dynasty ended with her. The new king of England was James I, a member of the Stuart family, which had ruled Scotland since 1371. His reign brought England and Scotland under one ruler for the first time in history. Although the Tudor period was relatively short, it left behind much of value. Tudor architecture still stands, Shakespeare's plays are still performed, and writers and directors turn to the era's fascinating characters time and again in books and films.

DEATH OF A QUEEN
Elizabeth's death was widely mourned. One thousand people walked in her funeral procession and tens of thousands turned out to see her final journey from Whitehall Palace to Westminster Abbey. The focal point of the procession was a life-like sculpture, or effigy, of the Queen on the top of the coffin. At Westminster Abbey, she was buried under the main altar of her grandfather Henry VII's chapel.

THE BRITISH EMPIRE
The foundations of the British Empire were laid during the Tudor period. Newfoundland had become Britain's first overseas possession in 1583, and initial colonies set up by Sir Walter Raleigh, although unsuccessful, laid the groundwork for permanent colonies to be established on the east coast of America. Crucially, the East India Company, set up with Elizabeth's support in 1600, had begun to build up the trading networks that would lead to the establishment of British rule over India and the growth of the largest empire the world has ever seen.

Designs for the union flag

UNION FLAG
The succession of James united the crowns of Scotland and England, although each kept its own parliament, religious institutions, and laws. Designs were drawn up combining the English and Scottish flags to represent the union. The new flag, first flown in 1606 and a forerunner of today's union flag, placed the two flags on top of one another.

THE KING
The crown passed to the son of Mary Queen of Scots, James VI of Scotland, who then also became James I of England. He had been king of Scotland for 36 years, since he was just one year old. James was witty and well-read, but he lacked his predecessor's charm and skill. He became known as a conceited and suspicious man, and he had difficulty being accepted in English society.

ORNATE ARCHITECTURE

A striking new style of architecture emerged in the Tudor period. Buildings were constructed from darkened, usually black wood beams, with which skillful craftsmen created decorative patterns. White-washed plaster was then used to fill in the structure to give a contrast to the dark timber, as shown here at Little Moreton Hall, Cheshire. During the early 20th century, this style of building was revived and was known as the mock Tudor style.

Poster for the 1966 film about Henry VIII, *A Man for all Seasons*

Poster for the 1998 film *Elizabeth*

UNIVERSAL ARTIST

The greatest artistic legacy of the Tudor age is undoubtedly the plays of William Shakespeare. Although 13 of his 37 plays were written after Elizabeth I's death, Shakespeare is always considered an Elizabethan playwright. His plays have never gone out of fashion and are still performed all over the world. This is because they contain so much universal insight into human nature, as well as having fascinating characters and clever plots.

THE TUDORS TODAY

Fascination with the drama, fashion, and language of the Tudor period continues today. Many of the main events and characters – Henry VIII and his six wives, the reign of Elizabeth I, Mary Queen of Scots' tragic life – have been kept alive through films, plays, and novels, as well as history books.

William Shakespeare (1564–1616)

A performance of Shakespeare's comedy *A Midsummer Night's Dream* in 2001

Index

Acknowledgements

Dorling Kindersley would like to thank: James Marks and Jody Harding of Hever Castle, Kent; The Knights of Royal England; The Cake Fairy; make-up artist Amanda Wright; Sheila Collins, Joe Conneally, Stefan Podhorodecki, Sarah Pownall, and Bradley Round for modelling; and Hilary Bird for the index.
The author would like to thank the design and editorial teams at DK for all their hard work.

P2 Reproduced by kind permission of His Grace the Duke of Norfolk, Arundel Castle, and of the Baroness Herries: cb; By permission of the Friends of Preston St Mary Church: tc; Hever Castle: cbr; P3 AKG London: tr; Bridgeman Art Library, London/New York: tl; P4 National Maritime Museum, London: reproduced by kind permission of the Chequers Estate cla; Courtesy of the Trustees of the V&A: tl; P6 Bridgeman Art Library, London/New York: Board of Trustees: National Museums & Galleries on Merseyside tc; British Library, London tl; National Portrait Gallery c; Philip Mould, Historical Portraits Ltd, London, UK cra, cra; Topham Picturepoint: cr, cr, bc. P7 Bridgeman Art Library, London/New York: Chelsea Physic Garden, London tc; Phillips, The International Fine Art Auctioneers, UK tl; Roy Miles Fine Paintings clb; The Stapleton Collection c; Victoria & Albert Museum, London, UK cl; Corbis: Jason Hawkes br; Dean and Chapter of York: reproduced by kind permission tr; P8 V & A, Bridgeman Art Library, London/New York: cra, clb, cal; P8-9 Topham Picturepoint: bc; P9 AKG London: tr; Ancient Art & Architecture Collection: cr; Bridgeman Art Library, London/New York: tr, clb; DK Images: British Library cra; Topham Picturepoint: cbl; P10 Bridgeman Art Library, London/New York: cal; DK Images: Museum of

English Rural Life cl; Museum of London cbl; P11 Bridgeman Art Library, London/New York: Hatfield House, Hertfordshire tr; Corbis: Eric Crighton c; P12 Hever Castle: bc; Historic Royal Palaces Enterprises: Crown copyright: Historic Royal Palaces: Courtesy of the Trustees of the V&A: cb, bl, cbl. P13 Bridgeman Art Library, London/New York: Ashmolean Museum br; Courtesy of the Trustees of the V&A: bl; P14 AKG London: British Library br; Bridgeman Art Library, London/New York: tl, cl, cr; Lebrecht Collection: bl; P15 AKG London: br; Bridgeman Art Library, London/New York: cl; The College of Arms: cra; P16 Bridgeman Art Library, London/New York: cra; DK Images: Science Museum tl; Asprey & Co bcl; DK Images: Science Museum tl; P16-17 P17 Bridgeman Art Library, London/New York: tcr; Bibliotheque Saint Genevieve, Paris crb; Corbis: by kind permission of the Trustees of the National Gallery, London bc; Mary Evans Picture Library: tr; Hever Castle: tc, cra; P18 Bridgeman Art Library, London/New York: Musee d'Orsay, Paris cla; DK Images: National Maritime Museum bl, bc; Wallace Collection tr; Mary Evans Picture Library: tl, cb; P19 Bridgeman Art Library, London/New York: cr, bc; DK Images: Wallace Collection cr; Warwick Castle cra; Topham Picturepoint: tr; Warwick Castle: c; P20 Bridgeman Art Library, London/New York: National Gallery of Art, Washington DC, USA tl; Hever Castle: bl; Topham Picturepoint: cr, cb, bcl; P20-21 Bridgeman Art Library, London/New York: Mark Fiennes / Sudeley Castle, Winchcombe, Gloucestershire, UK; P21 Bridgeman Art Library, London/New York: The Stapleton Collection ca; Hever Castle: br; Topham Picturepoint: tr, cla; P22 Corbis: Archivo Iconografico cla; Gianni Dagli Orti tl; Rex Features: bc; P23 Bridgeman Art Library, London/New York: Archives Charmet/Bibliotheque Mazarine, Paris, France cra;

The Stapleton Collection bc; DK Images: British Library cl; Topham Picturepoint: tc; P24-25 Bridgeman Art Library, London/New York: National Portrait Gallery, London, UK; The Stapleton Collection tr; The Trustees of the Weston Park Foundation tl; P25 Bridgeman Art Library, London/New York: Guildhall Library, Corporation of London, UK tc; Corbis: Adam Woolfitt cl; DK Images: tr; Glasgow Museum cdb; Museum of Order of St. John b; Sonia Halliday Photographs: F.H.C. Birch crb; P26 AKG London: clb; P27 Bridgeman Art Library, London/New York: Kunsthistorisches Museum, Vienna, Austria c, crb; The Berger Collection at Denver Art Museum, USA bc; Corbis: Hulton-Deutch Collection cla; Museum Of London: c; P28 Bridgeman Art Library, London/New York: National Portrait Gallery, London, UK bl; Mary Evans Picture Library: c; P29 Bridgeman Art Library, London/New York: tr, bcl; Christie's Images, London, UK cl; Giraudon/Louvre, Paris, France cr; British Library: t ; P30 Ancient Art & Architecture Collection: M&J Lynch; Bridgeman Art Library, London/New York: tl; Hamberg Kunsthalle, Hamburg, Germany cb; Mark Fiennes/Helmingham Hall, Suffolk, UK bc; National Maritime Museum, London: reproduced by kind permission of the Chequers Estate cla, ca; P31 Bridgeman Art Library, London/New York: Burghley House Collection, Lincolnshire, UK cra; Lambeth Palace, London, UK c; The College of Arms: t; By permission of the Friends of Preston St Mary Church: crb; Tophoto : bc; P32 Museum Of London: cl; P34 The British Museum: MI 116-48 clb; DK Images: Natural History Museum tl; Courtesy of the Trustees of the V&A: tl; P35 Bridgeman Art Library, London/New York: tc, br; St Faith's Church, Gaywood, Norfolk, UK c; Yale Center for British Art, Paul Mellon Collection, USA tcr; DK Images: Natural History Museum cla; Courtesy of the Trustees of the V&A: cb; P36 DK Images:

National Maritime Museum tl, tl; P36 National Maritime Museum, London: cl; P36-37 Getty Images: Clive Mason; P37 Bridgeman Art Library, London/New York: Ashmolean Museum bcr; National Portrait Gallery of Ireland, Dublin, Eire tl; DK Images: British Museum tr, Charlestown Shipwreck & Heritage Centre; Museum Of London: cla; Topham Picturepoint: British Museum c; P38 AKG London: Victoria and Albert Museum bl; Bridgeman Art Library, London/New York: c; Corbis: Michael Nicholson cl; Sandro Xannini br; Wolfgang Kaehler tl. P39 Reproduced by kind permission of His Grace the Duke of Norfolk, Arundel Castle, and of the Baroness Herries: tl; Bridgeman Art Library, London/New York: cl; Mary Evans Picture Library: br; Public Record Office: cra; Tophoto : cb; Courtesy of the Trustees of the V&A Picture Library: tcr; P40 DK Images: Mary Rose Trust cl; National Maritime Museum c; P40-41 Bridgeman Art Library, London/New York: Society of Apothecaries; National Portrait Gallery, London, UK tl; National Maritime Museum c; P41 Courtesy of the Trustees of the V&A: Mr D.P. Naish cr; P42 Bridgeman Art Library, London/New York: British Library crb. 42 British Library: ca. 42 Mary Evans Picture Library: tc, clb, tcl, tcr. 43 AKG London: Bibliotheque Nationale, Paris tc; P43 Bridgeman Art Library, London/New York: British Library tcl; DK Images: Weald and Downland Open Air Museum cl; P44 AKG London: tl; P44-45 Knights of Royal England: bc; P45 Bridgeman Art Library, London/New York: tc; P46 Corbis: Gianni Dagli Orti bc; DK Images: National Maritime Museum tl; National Library Of Scotland: The Trustees of the National Library of Scotland cr; P46-47 British Library; P47 Corbis: Bettmann c; Robbie Jack bc; Robert Estall tl; P47 Moviestore Collection: cl; Rex Features: Everett cal.

All other images: © Dorling Kindersley
For further information see www.dkimages.com